HOW TO SAVE A DYING RELATIONSHIP

Simple And Proven Techniques For Saving Any Sick Or Dying Relationship

KATHRYN RYCHES

INTRODUCTION

We've all had a fair share of dying, strained and broken relationships. Or we are presently in a relationship where all the sparks are gradually fading off and we wish there was something that we could do to help make it better.

Building any kind of relationship takes a lot of time and effort. You should not be deceived by all these glamor magazine stories and thrilling romance series, where sour relationships get better in minutes and with just a kiss.

This is reality, and in our world, things tend to be a little bit different and tough. Here we really feel pain and hurts, we share feelings and the bad emotions we feel do not just disappear with just a kiss.

But then, because we feel these things and have misunderstanding and complexities in our everyday relationship life, does not mean both parties in a relationship. Should part ways. There is always a way to go about reviving dying relationships. There is always a way you and your partner can bring back the spark in your relationship

CHAPTER ONE

The Relationship

Friendship, dating, or any other kind of relationship begins with an agreement of two persons, sometimes these agreements do not happen at once, but then, there is always an agreement. These relationships are beautiful things that involve physical, emotional, sexual, and sometimes spiritual intimacy. You should bear in mind that not all beautiful intimate relationships are sexual.

How Does It Work?

In a relationship, a lot of things are necessary to make it work, although not all of them would be necessarily found in all relationships. It is important to note that the more of them that are found in your relationship, the better your relationship life would be.

Intimacy

Intimacy involves the feeling of liking or loving someone and would most times result in physical expression characterized by romance, sexual activity, the feeling of being together, and other passionate endeavors.

We generally have the tendency to want to feel loved, wanted, and cared for. And most relationships are based on these factors.

Love

This is a feeling of strong affection for someone, it is classified as one of the strongest feelings man has ever felt. A relationship where both partners love each other tends to last longer and provides bliss and happiness to both persons involved.

Respect

Generally, it is a rule of thumb for mutual respect to be found in a thriving relationship for acceptance to follow. We tend to seek respect from people around us, no matter our age; talk more of the person with whom we have a relationship. This includes friendship, dating, and sibling relationships.

Acceptance

For a relationship to work, both parties must be willing to accept the other person wholeheartedly, this includes acceptance of both their perfection and flaws.

Commitment

From respect, comes full acceptance, then commitment. For a relationship to thrive both parties must be committed to each other and the working of the relationship.

Commitment involves total devotion to a cause or someone. Although this is not present in all relationships, it is necessary to note that successful partnerships/relationships are built on some form of commitment.

Relationships without commitment tend to drift away after a while. In a strong institutionalized relationship like marriage, most people would seek commitment from their partner before going on with their marriage.

Trust

This is a firm belief of reliability entrusted in someone or something. Trust is developed over time in a relationship when each partner must have built up credibility to earn the trust.

For relationships to thrive and last, it must be founded on trust. When two or more people trust themselves, things automatically become easier to do, goals are passionately pursued without fear and there is less reason for arguments, overthinking, and squabbles.

Relationships and partnerships require trust for both parties to effectively communicate, respect, and believe in each other.

Passion

Loving is not the only thing necessary in a relationship. Passion is direly needed, especially in dating and marriages. Passion is what makes partners in a relationship not to get tired of making sacrifices for each other, to take up challenges when things are rough.

It is important to note that passion is a fleeting feeling and can easily be spent as easily as it comes. In a thriving relationship, passion is built every day. It becomes a deliberate act after the first phase goes away.

Humans are wired to get distracted easily, especially with too many beautiful things and people surrounding our everyday lives. To make a relationship last longer, both parties must decide to love passionately and renew their passion every day.

Openness

Relationships work when there are no dark and secret corners. This is to avoid suspicions and double-minded. Openness is important in terms of effective and efficient communication, which is a necessity in our day to day activity in every relationship.

Relationships where partners hide secrets tend to grow to become a relationship built on suspicion and fear of the unknown. It is important to talk and communicate freely with your partner. Being open helps to build trust and Intimacy.

Loyalty

This is a strong feeling of devotedness to someone or a cause. A relationship that works has partners who are faithful and devoted to each other. The quality of being loyal serves as a glue to help hold your relationship and help you avoid unnecessary distractions that might bring about loss of trust from your partner.

Support

Supporting each other in a relationship is fundamental to the growth of the relationship. People in a relationship that do not receive support from their partner tend to seek support and validation elsewhere and this could damage the relationship.

Support can come in the form of emotional, financial, spiritual, and physical assistance.

Sacrifice

Relationships are built on sacrifice. Sacrifice involves forgoing things or people in order to make peace or pacify someone. Relationships where both partners make sacrifices for each other tend to be more successful than others

CHAPTER TWO

The Problem (What Does Not Work)

All relationships begin with one of the following traits listed in the previous chapter. If it doesn't then it does not become a relationship worth the effort.

In the long run, partners who are in a relationship would begin noticing some other diverse traits of their partner which they didn't know of before now. Some of these traits are unlikeable and least expected and when not properly handled can lead to problems in the relationship.

Here are some problems that might occur in a relationship as a result of differences in your partner's behavioral pattern:

Neglect

Partners in a relationship might have entirely different lifestyles, careers, and pursuits. One person might possess an outgoing personality while the other person might be an introvert. One might be a career person, ambitious and high flying, the other might not necessarily be overly ambitious.

This difference has been known to cause neglect among partners in a relationship. It is possible that one partner might unintentionally or intentionally neglect the need of the other partner and this might lead to problems in the relationship.

Abuse

This revolves around unwarranted use of force or other less violent means by one partner in a relationship to achieve their desires and wants.

Abuse in a relationship might not compulsorily be physical abuse; both emotional blackmail, verbal and psychological abuse are inclusive. All forms of abuse that may arise in a relationship would have adverse effects on the relationship and might cause severe damage.

Infidelity

This is a major cause of problems in relationships. Infidelity does not necessarily have to be a situation where one partner is sexually cheating on their significant other.

In relationships, other forms of infidelity might occur. This includes emotional and physical connections with another person other than your partner and these can lead to partners straying away from their significant other.

Poor Communication Habits

A partner can later notice that the other person does not have good communication habits and tends to find it difficult to communicate feelings of love, desires, wants, and needs.

This can adversely affect the relationship as feelings that are not expressed, especially the bad ones like anger would eventually build up and explode in the wrong way at the wrong time causing problems in the relationship.

Difference in Vision and Goals

Two people who fall in love can have different lifestyles and careers, but it is important that their visions align and that they are pursuing a common goal.

If you and your partner do not have a common futuristic goal, there is a larger likely risk of problems occurring sooner than later.

Emotional and Mental Health Issues

Partners with unresolved issues either from their past relationship or from a loss or unpleasant life experience, who carry the hurt and pain, tend to hold back from loving, or might not be able to give their best in a relationship due to the trauma associated with such experiences.

Partners who have certain underlying psychological and mental issues that can range from mild anxiety and depression to serious mental disorders would also experience a lot of problems that could destabilize the relationship.

Isolation

Although periods of cocooning is a normal thing in a relationship, where partners seek time and space to be alone, to get to bond better, to create special and fond moments. But then, staying away from family and friends for a long time, in a bid to get more 'alone - time' can lead to problems in the relationship.

Total isolation might be caused by fear and insecurities and would normally be initiated by one partner. This would lead to problems if the other partner wants a breath of fresh air and could amount to a breakdown.

Low Self Esteem

This is one of the major reasons for fear and insecurities in a relationship. When a partner is having feelings of not being 'love - worthy' due to some reasons, perhaps a certain health condition or a financial crisis. It is possible that their self-confidence and ego level might drop. They might begin to feel clingy and unnecessary insecure and this can lead to problems in the relationship.

Suspicions

A secretive partner is one who doesn't share feelings, information, details of their whereabouts, etc. These kinds of activities would bring up feelings of suspicion in the other partner, and feelings of suspicion would eventually lead to disbelief, distrust, and a breach of confidence amongst partners.

Control

As humans, we normally fall into the category of people having dominating behavioral traits, submissive behavioral traits, and persons who fall in between the specter.

Relationships where one partner is a control freak and the other partner has the same behavioral traits would barely last.

Relationships where one partner has the dominant factor and the other person has the submissive trait, but the person with the dominant trait has no check for his behavior would become tiring for the other partner.

Nobody likes to be controlled so much as to lose their will of doing things and having someone who is a control freak would mostly lead to problems in the relationship.

Broken Trust and Loyalty

A breach of trust caused by any of the above reasons would mostly bring problems in a relationship and can eventually lead to a relationship failure. With a break in trust, the motivation to continue is lost and if it is not fixed, a breakup will occur.

Loyalty is breached when a partner breaks the beliefs of faithfulness present in the relationship. This would definitely cause problems in the relationship.

CHAPTER THREE

Creating Better Relationships (What Will Work)

The above-listed causes of problems are common in most relationships, and at least, one or more are the cause of your dying relationship.

Creating a better relationship is something that both partners in the relationship have to be intentional about. If you notice your relationship is heading towards a pit, and you are the only one putting effort into making it work, it might barely work.

Both partners should sit together and decide to make strides in making the dying relationships work.

Here are steps to put into action to help you build a better and lasting relationship with your partner and bring the lost spark:

Forgive

A dying or strained relationship is caused by one or two issues or challenges that both parties have left unresolved. These things hurt and would have built up as bad emotions now acting against the formerly sweet flow of love in the relationship.

Partners who are ready to build back a dying relationship must first let go of these hurts and pain and must forgive each other wholeheartedly.

It is necessary not only to forgive your partner but also to forgive yourself. Forgiveness might appear difficult and unlikely, especially if it involves very vital things like a breach of trust and loyalty. But it is possible to let go of the hurt and love again.

Do it!

Address The Mistakes

Hurt does not just go away. Trust is not just broken and repaired at once as seen in movies. These things take time and they do not just solve themselves.

Partners in a relationship should sit and talk at length. Try to find out the source of the problem and talk about how to solve them. It is ok to be vulnerable, after all, this is your partner. Be open and apologize if you are the one at fault.

Spend Time With Each Other

Bonds are built and rekindled when two persons spend quality time together. Spending time with your partner can help you reconnect, communicate more, and eventually a way to go about solving your problems.

Spending time with your partner does not necessarily end at being together in a place, it includes doing things together, eating out, going on a vacation. Just anything that gives the opportunity for both of you to spend more time together.

Communicate Effectively

Poor communication is the major reason for a dying relationship. Therefore, to save a dying relationship, both partners in the relationship must develop strategies to enhance their communication skills.

Effective communication habits include good listening techniques, asking relevant questions, knowing when to interrupt or allow the other person to rant, etc. Both partners should listen to podcasts and read books that would help them communicate better, especially if poor communication habits are among the reasons for their relationship taking a downturn.

Perform Daily Acts Of Kindness

Another way to revive a dying relationship and fight against the habits that are killing it is to perform daily acts of kindness to your partner for no particular reason.

You should buy gifts, open the car door and show more kindness than you've been showing before. Whatever you can do to show more kindness, you should do them, as it would help you create a better relationship life.

Commit To Make The Relationship Works

To make a relationship work, both partners must be resolute and make firm decisions to make it work and commit to it.

If the commitment to make the relationship work is being undertaken by only one person, the relationship would be one-sided and this might even bring more problems. It is necessary that both parties be involved to make it work.

Set Boundaries

As much as being mushy, soft, and sweet in a relationship is important. It is also important that each individual set rules and boundaries that guide the relationship. It is necessary to be clear about what you want and what you stand for, to avoid had I known scenario. Set rules for your partners and for yourself as well and keep to it.

It is also important to put into consideration your individual strengths and weaknesses while setting these boundaries so that you don't set some rules that are beyond expectations and cause more problems.

Show Affection

We've been taught to agree that public display of affection is only common for 'puppy love', that is, for relationships that would have a lower percentage of chances to last long. This opinion has drastically made most couples transition from 'holding hands couple' to couples walking together, but with a large chasm between them.

Showing affection in a relationship, even in public places would help couples more in a relationship, it helps portray the image of being 'an item'. It brings out the thrills and joy of losing oneself in another. This show of affection helps build back bonds.

You should also note that this does not only include public display of affection but also frequently telling your partner that you love them when you are together alone.

Bath In The Shower

Aside from sex, bathing together with your partner is a major way you can rebuild physical intimacy. Bathing together with your partner provides both of you opportunities to create beautiful moments and make physical connections.

It is a special feeling to be naked and private with someone. This could also help reaffirm your love for each other. You should do it frequently, at least thrice a week to help build back your dying relationship.

Make Passionate Love

Sexual connection is a deep-seated kind of engagement between partners in a relationship and if both partners in a relationship still want to have sex with each other despite the state of the relationship, then this is a strong signal that both parties are deeply bonded and the effort to make the work is worth it.

Both partners should utilize this opportunity to make passionate love and try to bring alive the deep connection, sweet memories, and special feelings that they both have. This would help in building back a dying relationship.

Give Assurance

There are times when you notice your relationship is struggling, it is important that both partners give reassuring words and perform reassuring actions to help the other partner understand that they are still there for them.

This is mostly relevant in the case of distrust, disloyalty, low self-confidence, and low self-esteem. Giving reassuring words and performing actions that your partner can see and believe that you are sorry and value their trust and would want to earn it back is important.

Stop Heeding To External Influences

Advice and suggestions from friends and family are necessary when we are confused and at crossroads. But then, it is important not to heed all advice, opinions, and suggestions as they mostly contradict each other and would generally put you into a bigger mess.

Although these people might mean well, they are not in your shoes and can only provide suggestions based on their past experiences or stories that might not be similar to yours. You are the only one who knows so much about your relationship and can provide the right answers.

The lesser the external influence in your relationship, the betting it will be for you and your partner. Making decisions from your heart is always the best when trying to build back a dying relationship.

Please note that this does not include advice and suggestions from a counselor or your personal practicing relationship expert.

Focus On The Good Part

It is normal to always think about what went wrong, to brood, and try to figure out where each person must have faltered. Most people dwell on the mistakes and wrongs their partner must have done and this would continually make them notice more flaws and mistakes.

When building back a dying relationship, it is important to focus on the good things that they have done or that they are doing as a way to bring back the lost spark in your relationship. Dwell on good memories and try to remove your partner's ill from your thoughts. This will help both of you.

Do Not Try To Change Your Partner

Oftentimes, we desire some particular traits from our partner and want to make them possess or do such things by all means possible. This overbearing attitude of trying to change your partner would definitely bring frustration.

You have to decide to accept your partner the way they are and not try to change them or fix their life. Accepting their flaws helps you to be able to accommodate their mistakes, helps you not to make a comparison of them with another person and this can help you save your relationship.

Change and Grow

Most times, the monotony in our relationship adversely affects our relationship. It is necessary that you try to change and spice things up a bit.

Change your sex positions, Go out for a different kind of adventure, Visit new places together, try out new food and find new and exciting ways to spend time and build a variety of memories.

This change also includes changing bad behaviors and habits that you are stuck on, and those ones your partner had always complained about. Changing and growing both physical, emotional, psychological, and otherwise would definitely help you build a better relationship.

Compromise And Make Sacrifices

The ability to accept flaws that you wouldn't have accepted, the ability to drop the ego, and do things you wouldn't have done for others, the willingness to go the extra mile for your partner is what compromise and making sacrifices entails.

This is important, as it would determine the success or failure of any relationship. To save your about to die relationship. It is necessary for each individual to put aside their personal wants (this doesn't mean you should entirely leave your own goal and dreams) in a bid to achieve the encompassing goal of the relationship.

Putting the wants of your partner first, makes the other person feel wanted, loved, and appreciated and can help build bridges in a relationship.

Surprises And Gifts

Surprises are a good way to jumpstart your relationship from a dying phase to a blooming phase. Surprises are sweet and memorable. We all want surprises, even if we do not always agree to it.

You can send gifts or send a hand-written letter or take each other on surprised dates. Adding surprising activities and gifts to your relationship would help you make your relationship better.

Talk About The Pain, Hurt, And Disappointment

Most people just want to work out their relationship without talking about the hurt and pain. Sweeping the hurt underneath the carpet doesn't necessarily make it go away, instead it would accumulate and probably explode someday.

Talking about the pain as much as you can till the other person who was hurt actually would let go is a sure way to let off steam and ease off the burden. And if both partners are willing to talk about everything, leaving no stone unturned, then they've achieved a major milestone towards back their dying relationship.

Don't Judge

 Once both partners get to start talking about the pain and hurt. There is always the temptation to point accusing fingers at each other and judge each other for the mistake and preceding trouble that unfolded.

It is important that partners in a relationship try to avoid the urge to blame or point accusing fingers. Try to listen and evaluate without trying to judge your partner. Concentrate on finding the problem and looking for a solution instead. This would help both partners to avoid a bigger mess.

Avoid Complaining

When things go sour, it is natural for humans to complain. In a relationship where things are going erstwhile, it is evident to notice complaints and murmurs.

When partners continue complaining, they would start noticing more flaws and reasons to complain. It is a vicious cycle and partners who want to build their relationships should try as much as they can to avoid complaints.

Instead of complaints, try to cover it up by showing more love to yourself and your partner and watch the positive effects of overlooking flaws bring spark back into your relationship.

It is also important to note that trying to avoid complaining should not stop both partners from pointing out the mistakes of the other if they notice one.

Evaluate Your Progress Together

The journey of building back a dying relationship is not a personal one. It revolves around both parties in a relationship. It is therefore necessary to check on the progress of the effort of you and your partner and try to assess the progress of whatever efforts both partners have been putting into making the relationship work.

You should try to notice where the other partner is lagging and encourage each other to do better.

Seek Counseling

It is necessary to seek counseling as an alternative resort to making your relationship work.

A relationship counselor or expert would help both partners identify problems that they never had noticed or put into consideration while trying to make the relationship better. Since the counselor is making suggestions and giving advice from a different perspective and from professional experience, it is likely to help build the relationship.

Also, if one partner is falling short of the effort being put to build the relationship, a counselor would be able to notice and proffer professional solutions and guidance. Generally, a counselor would help partners in a dying relationship build themselves up by providing psychological support and routine activities that would treat hurt, and help heal the relationship.

CHAPTER FOUR

Making It Last

Now that you've been able to identify the cause of the problem in your relationship and you've learned how to build back a dying relationship by doing what works. It is now time to make your relationship better and make it last longer. Taking steps to make your relationship last is very important as most partners might leave off doing what they did to bring back the spark, and this might lead to another breakdown.

To avoid this vicious cycle of losing the spark in your relationship, lighting it up again, and having problems immediately afterward, both partners must take deliberate steps in establishing their love and guarding their relationship.

Here are some steps to take to make sure your relationship does not lose its spark again:

Compare and Affirm Your Individual Love Languages

To make your relationship last longer and become sweeter, each partner should be able to speak to the soul of the other. This communication can be done if partners in a relationship can effectively speak the love language of each other.

There are five major love languages that people use to communicate love and express feelings, each individual has a unique language. The five languages include:

- Physical Touch
- Acts of service
- Giving and receiving gifts
- Word of affirmation
- Spending quality time

It is important for partners in a relationship to discuss and understand each person's love languages so that they can be able to speak directly and effectively to each other's soul.

Couples should compare, affirm and try to indulge in acts that encapsulate the message of love to one another.

Nurture Friendship

It is important that friendship is nurtured in a relationship. Being in love is not enough, partners in a relationship should also try to become friends with each other as this would foster a better and greater relationship life.

Be Better

Now the problem has been taken care of and the relationship appears to be taking a smooth sail. It is important to note that those flaws that caused the first error might still be there.

Each partner in the relationship should put in deliberate effort to make sure that they become better in the relationship. You could attend relationship seminars, listen to podcasts and try reading books, it can help.

Believe in your partner

It is possible that you might have lost faith in your partner, but then, it is important you see the good part of your partner. If they were willing to go through making themselves better. You should try to understand that they have good interests and believe in them. Not believing in your partner might even result in more problems later.

Be there for them

Each individual in the relationship should try as much as possible to be there for their partners as this is important to help the relationship grow.

Learn how to Share

Maybe holding secrets had been the reason why suspicion and distrust had surfaced in the relationship. You should endeavor to learn how to share. This includes sharing your secrets, fears and pains, etc.

Be true to your words:

You must have made good decisions to become better, you probably might have set rules for yourself and your partner. It is important that you are true to your words.

Express Appreciation and Gratitude:

Appreciation and gratitude are one of the greatest factors for sustainability in a relationship. It is important that each partner make the other understand how grateful they are to have them in their life.

It is also necessary to show appreciation for everything and nothing at the same time. A person who is appreciated would always want to do more.

Create a couple of bucket list

Another way to bring more life into your relationship is to create a bucket list. A couple of bucket list would contain all the things you wish to do for a certain period of time.

You can create a bucket list for five years and try to do them. This would make sure you do not run out of fun activities to keep each other smiling and happy.

CHAPTER FIVE

Conclusion

Saving a dying relationship might take some effort on the part of each partner, but then, we now know that it is possible. It requires no rocket science technique, but the passion, determination, and dedication of each partner in a relationship.

Identifying the problem first is the key, knowing how to tackle it comes next, then actually doing them would help you save your dying relationship.

It is also important to note that as much as you want to save a relationship, there are some relationships that you should cut off and get along with life.

If you see a good number of the following things listed below, then it is high time you pack up and leave.

If your needs are not being met

 If your partner cares so little about meeting your needs consistently over a period of time, with no particular reason, then it is a signal that you need to leave.

If you are always scared to ask for more

 If you notice that there are certain things you need or want but then you are scared to ask, either because you know your partner wouldn't heed or they would constantly make you feel as if you are bugging them. Then this is another sure signal.

If all friends and family totally disagree

It is ok not to listen to external influence, but sometimes if everyone is giving you a head up, you should stand back and try to notice why.

If your partner is abusive

 Irrespective of which kind of abuse, physical, emotional, or psychological.

If your relationship brings you more pain than joy

There are relationships that are entirely toxic and whenever one gets to think about it, they lose their smile. If you are in such, it is high time you begin to heed to the signs.

If your partner wants you to change

Nobody should try to change you, you are special already. Someone can only want to make you better. If your partner begins to nudge you to change everything about you. This is another sign.

If you continually justify your partners wrongdoings

 Because we love it so much, we tend to cover our eyes to our partner's fault. If you continually find yourself giving excuses for your partner's shortcomings and can not even bring yourself to talk about it. Then maybe it is time for you to confirm other signs and move.

If your partner is putting little or no efforts

If you notice that you are putting in the bulk of the work and your partner is doing little or nothing to make the relationship better, then it is time to move ahead

If your fundamental beliefs and goals are different

If both partners in the relationship no longer share the same beliefs and goals, there is a higher possibility of

both partners having a clash than a kiss. You should
move ahead.